Glasgow

FROM THE EYE IN THE SKY

Glas

FROM THE EYE

gOW
IN THE SKY

Text by

IAN
ARCHER

Photographs by

DOUGLAS CORRANCE

MAINSTREAM
PUBLISHING

RADIO CLYDE

First published in Great Britain in 1988
reprinted in 1989 by
MAINSTREAM PUBLISHING COMPANY (EDINBURGH) LTD
7 Albany Street, Edinburgh EH1 3UG

ISBN 1 85158 168 5 (cloth)

British Library Cataloguing in Publication Data
Corrance, Doug
Glasgow: from the eye in the sky
1. Scotland. Strathclyde Region. Glasgow
I. Title II. Archer, Ian
941.4'4430858

Design by JAMES HUTCHESON

Typeset in Bodoni by Bookworm Typesetting, Edinburgh.
Colour separation by Marshall Thompson, Edinburgh.
Printed in Great Britain by Butler & Tanner Ltd, Frome, Somerset

CONTENTS

The pictures here are by Doug Corrance, a master craftsman with a good, perceptive eye. He has brought to Glasgow a couple of qualities. For a start, he does not live here, so he sees the city as others see it. And he points his camera at the place from oblique, sly and occasionally wicked angles. The result is a civic portraiture of the highest order.

Glasgow is all things to all its people. The shared experiences in this city count for no more than the diversity of life within it. It is a long way from Kelvinside to Castlemilk and that has nothing to do with geography.

Symbolically, it is cut in half by a river which ebbs and flows. In the last few years, salmon have started to return to the Clyde, a sign that the waters are cleaner and more inviting. The same might well be said about Glasgow itself.

The words here are about a New Glasgow, but it's an elusive place to pin down. It is not about the new buildings which planners and architects have given us, not before time. Or the way they have scraped the dirt off the old ones. It is not about the flashy and fashionable image which the city now possesses, thanks to the "Glasgow's Miles Better" campaign, much as that raised the morale of the citizenry.

The New Glasgow is no more than today's Glasgow, the way it is now. It is simply an accident of birth which makes anyone a Glaswegian and it is quite often simply necessity which keeps him in the place where he was brought up. But to be born and to live in Glasgow as of this moment is a privilege to be shared.

FOREWORD

Captain George Muir at the controls of "The Eye In The Sky" every morning, as he reports on traffic conditions, occasionally becomes almost lyrical in describing the City beneath him. For most of us a trip in a helicopter is a rare and, in the right conditions, an unforgettable experience. It offers, literally, a new angle on familiar landmarks.

This book, through the camera lens of Douglas Corrance and the prose of Ian Archer, tries to portray the Glasgow of today from the air and the ground. I believe it succeeds. It also offers a glimpse of some of the spectacular surrounding countryside giving Glasgow one of the finest settings of any city in Europe. I hope that the increasing number of visitors to the City will find this a welcome souvenir to take back to friends and relatives – and persuade them to come next time.

Even before its spectacular growth in the middle of the last century, Glasgow had suffered at least one major recession with the collapse of the tobacco trade after the American War of Independence. But the City bounced back and it is good to be alive in the Glasgow of the 1980s when something of that indomitable spirit is discernible again. Huge problems still remain but the will to tackle them is there and, more important, the confidence that we can do it.

Many of the photographs in this book testify to the tremendous sense of confidence which must have inspired many of the great buildings in the City. Now that the industrial grime deposited by previous generations has been removed, they are revealed in their original splendour. More important, perhaps, they are rivalled by some recent additions – the Garden Festival, the Burrell Collection, Princes Arcade and many more. Some, like the vast new St Enoch Centre are

RADIO CLYDE.

still in the process of construction. And it is certain that the visitor to Glasgow five years from now will find even more to enthuse about.

Many photographs in the book also help to show the River Clyde itself in a new light. It is no longer an important industrial artery providing the key to the City's industrial wealth. The Firth of Clyde has long been recognised as one of the finest sailing areas in Europe but perhaps the building of the new Bell's Bridge as a pedestrian link across the River signals a rebirth of that part of the River which flows through the City itself as an important leisure facility.

As part of our 15th Birthday celebrations, Radio Clyde is happy to assist with the publication of this book and hopes that it will provide many hours of enjoyment to all who read it.

James Gordon
Glasgow, 1988

The New
GLASGOW

Glasgow? The man thought. It's just like New York, with a small 'n' and a small 'y', just like Manhattan." It was the recurring statement round every corner of a city which isn't what it used to be. But why new york?

By some process of elimination, it becomes clearer. The city isn't like London with its pomp and circumstance. It certainly isn't like Paris or Madrid. Germany is bits and pieces, old and new. Rio is too hot. Buenos Aires comes close. What Glasgow mostly isn't like is Edinburgh – new york will do.

It was once the Second City of an Empire, on which the sun set very quickly. Then it became a very bad town, feared rather than respected. Like any other place, if you were born there, you took it for granted. Suddenly, it flowered and came into bloom. New architects made grand buildings. Painters painted and writers wrote and singers sang. A smile of comedians told stories about it. It was almost on the verge of being fashionable, but resisted such flattery.

Like all great cities, Glasgow is a collection of villages which have agreed reluctantly to live together as best they can. Through the middle of it runs a great river which jointly separates and unites it. At the moment Glasgow is celebrating itself and its citizens are trying hard not to let anyone know they might just be a wee bit proud of the good old place.

I was walking along a Glasgow street not so long ago as Rod Stewart and Elton John were emerging from a pub. As they walked out, a bunch of local lads spotted them. In other cities, they might have been greeted with condescension, they might have been ignored, they might have been fawned over with great respect. Anywhere else, something would have happened. Our guys took a quick glance, realized who they were, nodded briefly, said, "Hi Rod, Hi Elt" and carried on walking. It was not so much a put-down, more a mark of respect. There was nothing special in the meeting, nor the men they had met. Just another Glasgow Saturday, and in any case, they were all paying to get into the same football match later on.

I was born here but lived away. We came every summer for our holidays and the grandness of Glasgow seemed very grand to a boy with big eyes. To pass over the Clyde on the way into Central Station as a train which had started in London finally slowed down and blew smoke back amongst the carriages was the child's entry into the paradise of a big city.

The taxi queue outside in Gordon Street . . . the tram going up the hill of Renfield Street . . . and all those people scurrying about. There were big Victorian buildings and newsvendors selling copies of so many papers which the city devoured. There would be the games in the backcourts, visits to the park, tea with relatives three up left in a wally close. No Mediterranean beach, the idyll for today's kid, ever had such romance.

It was a noisy and dirty city. The trams clattered. Little workshops made things and the presses beat a steady rhythm. It was a city with a cinema on every corner and a dance hall just down the road. Loch Lomond was on its doorstep. The rest of the world seemed a long way away. It was, quite simply, despite where you lived, home.

And still is, though utterly changed.

Thirty years ago, it was possible to take a Clyde Steamer all the way from the Broomielaw to Campbeltown and back in the same day. The vistas of the Clyde were the attraction which brought visitors from all over the world to do just that. But the best bit was the start. The welders and riveters in shipyards like Harland and Wolff made enormous noises which ricocheted from one bank of the river to the other. The small ferries at places like Govan and Renfrew pottered backwards and forwards. A city was busy at hard and dirty work. Downriver, older people pointed out where the *Queen Elizabeth* had been launched into an inlet specially created to receive her vast bulk. After those excitements, the rest of the day was dull.

Ten years later, the city had lost its nerve. The big industries were fleeing to other countries if they were needed at all. City tenements, the very basis of Glasgow's communal life, were falling into disrepair.

They had carved a very necessary motorway straight through the city
and over the river but beside it and underneath it some of those villages
had completely disappeared. Woodside was falling apart, Finnieston
and Anderston had gone. The cinemas and the dance halls had
diminished. They had decanted thousands out to bleak estates, or
schemes, like Easterhouse and Drumchapel and Castlemilk and then
wondered why folks who had lived shoulder to shoulder in the city did
not like the barracks on the outskirts. Whole new towns like East
Kilbride were created as if short-distance migration would bring a New
Jerusalem.

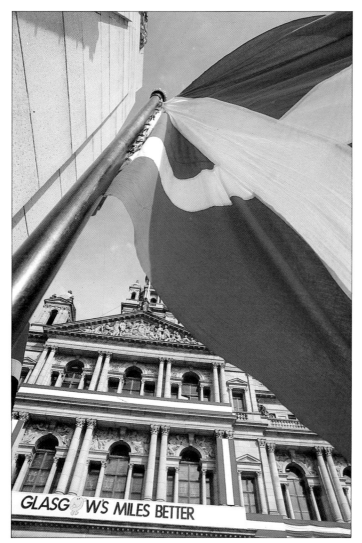

It tested pride in a home town. It was possible to escape into some kind of nostalgia for a life which wasn't very good. Young people drifted southward. People lost their lives in fires at warehouses and on the steps of an out-of-date football stadium. The city's artistic life was to be found in a small West End ghetto, where artists would bite and claw at each other. Glasgow never became a bad place but for a while it was very ordinary.

Quite how it changed – and how it changed so quickly and dramatically – remains something of a mystery. There was a general belief that blah, blah, something had to be done. There was the whole

massive problem, which, on its own, would have defeated many other cities, of what to do with its East End, the bad patch. What won the day for Glasgow was a negative virtue. It refused to retreat into dogmatism.

This is very much the plain man's view. The average Glaswegian remains blissfully uninterested in the working lives, philosophies or even the expenses of his locally elected representatives, which is another way of saying that he's quite prepared to let that lot up at the City Chambers get on with it just as long as they don't bother him with pious incantations or put the rents up too much.

There are many myths about Glasgow which are just that, myths. It was never the case that thousands of citizens were afraid to go out at night because they would be met by thousands of other members of the city who were carrying razors and broken bottles in the same numbers as Londoners swing umbrellas. Central Station was never Central Park. This was always quite a peaceful city with some well-known pockets of resistance to pacificism or law and order.

Neither was it the case that Glasgow was all Red Clydeside, one huge cell of Marxists and Trots and Stalinists who thought their duty in life was to declare Glasgow an independent socialist republic and then turn the guns on neighbours who had not seen the light. Its working-class leaders – Maxton, Gallagher and the others – wanted, with hindsight, little more than decent treatment for ordinary men and women in a working-class city. If there was a difference between Glasgow and the rest of Great Britain, it was found in the need to establish an independent spirit of purpose.

So no dogma, just hard work. If some project was considered worthy of Glasgow, it was not placed in the centre circle and then kicked around like a political football. There was to be improvement, not ideology. We allowed our politicos to have their occasional ritual wrangles, but these were never serious or divisive. Too many people would never let them get away with it anyway.

It all began to come together in a million tiny and not so tiny ways. Glasgow got its own Radio Station which treated Glasgow as the centre

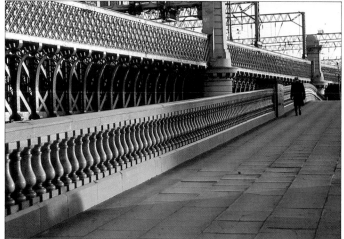

of the world. Billy Connolly, the comedian, not only made us laugh at ourselves, but made others laugh with us and not at us. Bill Forsyth went out and made a very tender film, *Gregory's Girl*, which was watched around the world and people saw that kids grew up in Glasgow just like they grow up in other parts of the world. Robert Miller cycled in the Tour de France. Sandy Lyle, the golfer, won Majors and his family came from not much more than a seven iron away from the city.

There was good opera and ballet. Rangers spent £10,000,000 on a new football ground. The council started doing up the tenements instead of knocking them down. The Clayson Report allowed Scots to drink round the clock and, in doing so with dignity and restraint, Glaswegians shook off their image as sots. The Pina Colada became the New Glasgow's answer to the whisky and half pint of beer – well, not quite.

Tourists began to arrive, rather than plotting their route over the Erskine Bridge towards the Highlands. Hotels opened and restaurants abounded.Simple Minds were the heroes of the disco set. The music journalists tried to compare Glasgow of the Eighties with Liverpool of the Sixties, a fanciful conjunction but still flattering. These are just a few instances – incomplete and highly selective – of how this one man watched Glasgow straighten its back, poke out its chest and look squarely in the eye of anyone who wanted to see it in the last decade.

What has not changed about Glasgow is its people. They are still the same crowd of pawky, ordinary, optimistic and unselfconscious men, women and children as they ever were. Glasgow celebrates Garden and Culture. Outsiders come to celebrate its citizens.

GEORGE

Captain George looks down from his Bell Jet Ranger helicopter, flying at 1,500 feet over the City of Glasgow. He is very fond of his bird, which he sometimes calls his budgie. Sometimes many people would like to strangle it. Shortly before eight o'clock every morning, he wheels it out of its cage at the SEC or Glasgow Airport to share the suffering of thousands of people on their way to work.

"That was Fleetwood Mac . . . and I express my envy for the Captain this morning 'cos at five past six the sun was just heading up, the sky was clear, heading to be a blue one too. It's a lovely morning, cold but fresh. It's a good description of Captain George, cold but fresh. In the Barr's Irn Bru Eye in the Sky. George, good morning."

On Radio Clyde, Dave Marshall's *Breakfast Show* is cranking Glasgow up for another busy day in the office. Captain George will look down upon motorists. They will look up, see him eyeing them from the sky and envy his freedom. In some sort of late 20th-century Utopia, they will give us all a budgie.

"Good morning, Dave. Good morning everybody, and yeah, I couldn't have put it better myself, Dave. It's gorgeous up here this morning. I think the real Glasgow expression would be 'a stoater'. It's an absolute stoater of a morning. I can see all the way over to the Firth of Forth. You can believe that, believe it or not. Shotts transmitter's away in the distance, the Pentland Hills, clear blue skies everywhere, absolutely gorgeous. Down on the roads, things are looking, well, not absolutely gorgeous, but . . . ."

Anything but. They are nose to tail coming over the Kingston Bridge, a legend in the new Glasgow patois – "Sorry I'm late, but the

traffic on the Kingston Bridge . . . ." They are bumper to bumper westbound on the M8 as the Townhead Interchange, more of a soft noodle than a spaghetti junction, takes its toll. The motorway that slashes through Glasgow looks from Captain George's eyrie just like any traffic system from Frankfurt to Oslo, Madrid to Munich, at the start of the working week.

George has travellers' tales to tell. One morning, there was a long tailback on the Maryhill Road, where a little white Escort had run out of puff. Hovering above the done-in set of wheels, he asked the passenger to get out and push it to the side of the road. The Clyde woman listener obeyed. The traffic started to move again. The lady looked up and gave him the same sign they would recognize from Frankfurt to Oslo, Madrid to Munich.

He also has a bird's eye view of a city as few have seen it. Even this early spring morning, the sun is up, but the mist still needs to be burnt away. His first stop is out over the city, all the way to Calderpark Zoo.

"See the house in the middle there, surrounded by water. That's the polar-bear house. And there he is, that's Winston the Bear," he says. The budgie tilts from side to side and flaps its wings to wish Winston a happy good morning: "Always comes out to see me, does Winston." It is one way, I suppose, of upping the Radio Clyde audience figures.

Captain George returns to the city. Down to the right is Easterhouse. It looks small, inoffensive. There is Park Gardens, from the air looking like a giant key which will unlock the city for you. The River Clyde meanders. The city centre looks like a small Manhattan, rectangular, efficient. Hampden Park, cut down to size, still looks enormous. Ibrox Park is square, tidy, colourful. The new St Enoch's development shines with steel and glass.

Captain George can see a city beneath a city. He points out the
remains of Roman forts. He plots the disappearing tracks of the city's
old railways. From this third dimension, it's clear that any city does not
just sprawl sideways, it's built up layer upon layer from the bottom,
like gateaux.

"Somebody once told me that Glasgow has more parks than any
other city in Europe – per capita, that is," he adds. From 1,500 feet,
airspeed just over 100 knots, the city's favourite colour is green.
Kelvingrove, Queen's Park, Ruchil, Rouken Glen, offset the reddish
grey of the tenements. Nestling inside the surrounding hills, Glasgow
was built expansively. "The West German ambassador was up the
other week," says George. "He said he had never seen a city as
beautiful." Of course ambassadors are trained and selected to make
just such remarks, but the man might just have been telling the pure
and unadulterated truth.

There is snow on the hills over on distant Arran. Just one chimney
belches out smoke on a city which gets cleaner every passing year. The

giant cranes stand like vultures over the dead shipyards. This is an odyssey.

And the traffic hasn't been too bad. By nine o'clock everything is moving. The wee suburban trains are gliding into Central Station. The Inter-City Expresses are limbering up for the long-distance dash to London. Winston has gone for a dip.

The budgie seems to have enjoyed his early morning work-out. Seen from the sky, Glasgow looks magical. The trick is to search out the splendour while looking upwards from the ground. Actually, it's not very difficult.

Before the New
G L A S G O W

Before there was a new Glasgow, there was an old Glasgow. Its history is vigorous, although not always distinguished. It grew from small beginnings to become – for a while – amongst the half dozen most important cities in the world. Its great days were short but remarkable. Most of all, Glasgow has been resilient.

With a cathedral founded in 1136 and a University in 1451, it can claim a certain antiquity. During the 17th century it grew from a population of only 5,000, which ranked 11th, to become the second biggest place in Scotland. Ships and the evil tobacco weed put it into the big league. The barons who ran the trade gave it a prominence on both sides of the Atlantic. Small boats, making perilous voyages, brought the stuff in. By 1771, Glasgow imported an incredible 46 million tons of tobacco from Virginia, North Carolina and Maryland. The port was black with ships. Only three million tons of that cargo stayed in a Britain united by the Act of Union in 1707. The rest went on to France and it was this trade which made the merchants rich. The shipowners, too, because they went the other way, carrying furniture, clothing, boots and glassware on ships which would otherwise have been empty. Tradesmen flocked to Glasgow to make artifacts for the New World.

It was still not a big place. When Daniel Defoe visited Glasgow at the same time, he damned with faint praise. "The most beautiful little town in Great Britain," he wrote.

During that same century, Adam Smith, author of *An Enquiry into the Nature and Causes of the Wealth of Nations*, was the Professor of Logic and Moral Philosophy at Glasgow University. He had only to look out of his window at the busy commercial life of the place to confirm his theories. When tobacco declined in its trading importance, cotton replaced it. It seemed as if the River Clyde and its natural estuary was all that Glasgow needed for its relative prosperity to continue without any problems.

There was one man who changed not only the city. Without exaggeration, he altered civilization. Born in 1736, James Watt developed the steam engine and gave birth to the industrial revolution. Precisely, he invented a method of condensing steam in a separate vessel which he kept cold. This stopped some three-quarters of the wastage of steam which earlier engines found to be the fatal flaw and, from that moment, the world changed.

When Henry Bell launched his steamship *Comet* in the Clyde, in 1811, it became the first boat of its type to take to open waters. It was appropriate that a city which had lived by the sea now had the means to make the new ships for the sea. Ten years later, 48 other steamships were under construction and so entered into the litany of the language the phrase "Clyde-built". Coal came from nearby Lanarkshire, and iron ore too. If Glasgow thought about it at all, it was at the centre of a new universe. People flocked here, and between 1791 and 1861 the population grew from a mere 67,000 to 448,000.

People – the ordinary folks – mattered little, of course. They were not as efficient as machines and, besides, they made trouble. In the 1820s Andrew Hardie, an ancestor of Keir Hardie, was hanged as the leader of a Glasgow uprising. Twenty years later Glasgow had to deal with the consequences of the great Irish potato famine. Some 50,000 of the starving fled eastwards across the water in appalling conditions at fourpence for the one-way trip to escape Ireland's deprivations.

In 1842 a railway line to Edinburgh was opened. In Glasgow they made carpets for the world, printed books and exported whisky. The great shipping lines were run from the city – the Glen Line to China, the Castle Line to the Far East and the Donaldson Line to Canada. When Glasgow, at the start of the century, had grown to a place of over one million people, only London and Paris outranked it in size throughout Europe. It was bigger than Berlin, Vienna or St Petersburg.

In the 19th century Glasgow continued to spawn remarkable men. In 1871, Tommy Lipton was a cabin boy on a steamer to New York. He came back to open a wee grocer's in Stobcross Street, buying

THE ART GALLERIES AT KELVINGROVE.

vegetables direct from farmers in Ireland. It was the start of his amassing a great fortune out of tea. He bought plantations and devoted his spare time in spending a fortune trying to win the Americas Cup for Great Britain. It was about the only endeavour in which he failed.

Greek Thomson was changing the architecture of the city, which the city did not always appreciate. Only a century later it needed the late Sir John Betjeman to advise Glaswegians to take their eyes off the pavement, look up at the city-centre buildings and glory in the fact that the place contained all that was best in Victorian civic and commercial architecture. Charles Rennie Mackintosh was designing, inside and out, his own art-deco style, a mixture of black functionalism combined with austere flourish. He remained, for 100 years, a prophet with little honour in his own city – a European before his time.

In this century there were the ships. As they were being built they rose as huge unpainted giants, towering above the tenements which surrounded the yards and which housed the men who had to work hard, skilfully, dangerously and dirtily to bring steel and iron to life. The *Aquitania*, the *Queen Mary* (No. 543) came from here. In 1940,

the *Queen Elizabeth* set sail for New York without undergoing trials, so great was the need for her bulk in the war effort. She carried 1,250,000 soldiers back and forth across an Atlantic infested with U-boats. On one memorable trip the *Queen Mary* carried 23,000 troops. Churchill left four times from the Clyde on hazardous journeys to meet President Roosevelt. There were warships too – the *Duke of York*, the *Howe* and the *Indefatigable*, dozens of smaller cruisers, frigates and minesweepers.

But the war was one last surge of pride. By 1951, Glasgow had surrendered its title as the Second City of the Empire to Birmingham. The population was beginning to duck under a million. Although there were to be big days, as when the *QE2* went down the slipway, Glasgow became a city in waiting.

Waiting for something to happen; waiting to see what would replace its heavy industry, no longer needed; waiting for its houses to be replaced; waiting to find out what Central Government had in mind for it; waiting for a new role. Then it stopped waiting and made things happen all over again.

PARK CIRCUS. IN A CITY OF STRAIGHT LINES, ONE PART OF IT BENDS.

GLASGOW'S WEST END.

THEM AND US

The average Glaswegian regards his betters with a mixture of scorn and disinterest. Especially those who have the temerity to want to govern the populace. After all, this place was once Red Clydeside, and even if the notion that the city was full of tens of thousands of Marxists all intent on the immediate overthrow of heinous capitalist pigs was as laughable then as now, there is nothing in the constitution which positively states that we must love our friendly neighbourhood councillors. Unless you want the drains fixed, of course.

Still, they are there and seem mostly to be good souls. They do their best. Each year they produce a little brochure about Glasgow which unfortunately does not knock the latest spy thriller off the bestseller shelves of the bookshops. But it deserves to be read, despite a prose style which makes the rules and regulations on the back of a bus ticket look decidedly racy. It's called *City Profile – the Facts and Figures about Glasgow*. This is its summary – with glossary.

With a 1986 population of 725,130, Glasgow is the largest of Scotland's District Councils. The population of the city is expected to fall to 694,984 by 1992, a decline of about 30,000. Despite the population decline, the number of households in the city is expected to increase substantially from 284,093 in 1985 to 298,480 in 1992, a rise of just over 14,000.

How can they be so accurate? If Rangers or Celtic win the European Cup in Lisbon in 1992, there will be a few thousand who go and never come back. The very thought that 30,000 Glaswegians will be scattered to the four winds, though, is deeply encouraging. They will

Previous Page
GEORGE SQUARE.

spread the gospel around Great Britain and the world, which will become more civilized. For the rest of us there should be more taxis to go round, although not when it is raining.

In 1986, the City's total housing stock stood at over 302,000 dwellings, which represents an increase of over 1,500 on the 1985 figure. Publicly rented housing comprises the greatest proportion of this stock. Although there is a notional surplus of housing, substantial needs remain unmet. There are still not enough good quality and attractive houses of suitable size, nor are there sufficient houses to meet specialized needs. Great strides, however, have been made in rebuilding and rehabilitation, especially in the inner city areas. Recent years have seen an increase in private house building in the City and the conversion of nineteenth century warehouses for residential use.

Getting on the housing list and then getting to the top of it was the Glaswegian's equivalent of the Duke of Edinburgh Award scheme. Truly, the Glasgow Housing Policy has often belonged to the Theatre of the Absurd. They pulled down wonderful tenements, demolished huge blocks of damp flats, built high-rises where no-one wanted to live. These were no joking matters. Now people like Mr Bovis, Mr Wimpey and Mr Lawrence do seem to be putting up nice wee places. Today's litany of necessary housing jargon includes Homesteading, Tenant Management Co-operatives, Community Trusts and Council House Sales. It is as fashionable to live in the built-in community of a tenement as it is to stay in a warehouse. I suppose, however, the warehouse is a better bet if you have a large family.

The number of jobs in the City has declined significantly over the last 10 to 15 years. Employment in Glasgow is now estimated at 326,000 compared to 364,000 in 1981 and 404,000 in 1978. Manufacturing industries have borne the brunt of this decline. It is the service industries such as banking/finance and retailing which now form the core of the City's economy and the thrust of new job generation. Developments in the service sector, while significant, have not offset the loss of traditional jobs. Despite a fall of 3,800 over the last year, unemployment remains high at 73,400 (20.5% of the economically active residents).

We know who's to blame for all that, don't we? I take it that an economically active resident is anyone who can make his hand stretch into his back pocket the day before the next Giro is due. We have, it

CITY CHAMBERS.

would seem, stopped building ships and turned into a city full of merchant bankers, although few have ever been spotted in Easterhouse. "Retailing" is a posh word for standing behind a counter watching the queues grow. Post Offices are a good training-ground for retailers.

> Glasgow is by far the largest shopping centre in Scotland, drawing trade from the whole of the Strathclyde Region and beyond. The City's shopping policy is geared towards encouraging new development within or adjacent to existing shopping centres. It is important to ensure that existing centres, which are, in general, the most convenient locations for all sections of the public to do their shopping, remain attractive and prosperous.

The best-known tailor in Glasgow, Slaters, is up a close in Howard Street at the back of the new St Enoch's development. It sells menswear to people beyond Strathclyde. Some of the signs are in Icelandic. The Icemen cometh for the same reasons as Glaswegians. The shop is full, friendly, and the prices are right. Not like the other places in Buchanan Street.

Tackling Glasgow's environmental problems is one of the Council's strategic objectives. With other agencies, the Council has established a number of environmental improvement programmes and policies for the protection of the countryside, conservation areas and listed buildings. Since 1975, great progress has been made in improving the environment of Glasgow, especially the inner city. As in other British cities, however, vacant land, often unsightly, continues to give rise for concern. When treated some provides opportunities for future development but where it is difficult to develop, landscaping is improving the general environment. Vacant buildings, too, where they can be suitably converted to modern needs are being brought back into use.

Actually Glasgow has 20 conservation areas and over 1,000 listed buildings. Psst . . . wanna buy one? You can adopt a statue or a fountain in a sponsorship scheme designed to clean them up. The Scottish Development Agency has spent £65 million on environmental improvement since 1977. The pity was that the trams were gone before they started. Anyway, all the money gives a brand new slant to the original Gaelic name for Glasgow which translated as a "Dear Green Place".

GEORGE SQUARE AND THE CITY CHAMBERS ARE THE HEART OF GLASGOW. YET NOBLE PILES HAVE NEVER BEEN ALLOWED TO OVERWHELM THE HUMAN SPIRIT. TODAY'S COUNCILLORS NEED ONLY TO LOOK AROUND THEM TO GLIMPSE THE HERITAGE THEY ARE CHARGED TO MAINTAIN AND IMPROVE.

Glasgow offers a wide and varied range of leisure and recreational facilities. The city holds its own horse show, festival of popular theatre, Mayfest, and an international jazz festival. In addition it is the home of the Scottish National Orchestra, Scottish Opera, Scottish Ballet and the Royal Academy of Music and Drama.

Which must make Glasgow the best place in the World for Lucinda Green MBE to watch the *Marriage of Figaro*. The odd 1,500,000 or so to go to watch football every year, by the way. And the Bay City Rollers came from Edinburgh.

Tourism is becoming increasingly important to the city's economy. In 1986, 1.7 million domestic tourists spent some £119 million in Greater Glasgow, which reflects the success of promotions like the "Glasgow's Miles Better" campaign. The development of new hotels and conference facilities bears witness to the City's growing share of the holiday and conference market.

Any Glaswegian can bear testimony to the tourist explosion. They are the ones in front of you in the bus queue being chatted up by the locals. They recommend staying at the Great Eastern Hotel and inform them that the Saracen's Head is a nice place for dinner.

In the academic yeare 1986-87, the City's two Universities and 12 further education colleges had 63,000 students. There are currently 93,000 pupils in the state comprehensive system and this is expected to rise to 99,000 by 1992.

This sounds as if the truancy officers have suddenly been put on piece work. Glasgow University possesses the best snooker tables in Glasgow. The city has always prided itself upon its literacy, though of course any relationship with the academic system is tenuous.

Glasgow has an extensive network of health and welfare facilities run by a variety of public, private and voluntary agencies and a number of these provide specialist services for areas well beyond the City's boundaries. Health Services are co-ordinated by the Greater Glasgow Health Board with 32 hospitals, providing beds for over 11,500 patients, 14 health centres and 51 clinics.

Glasgow tops many charts – British, European and World – for the incidence of coronary heart disease and lung cancer. It is our own fault, we should live better. Our doctors and nurses show far more patience with us than we deserve.

Glasgow has an integrated transport network located at the centre of the Scottish road and rail systems. Glasgow's motorway system provides rapid access from the City Centre to Scotland's populous central belt and beyond for business, freight and commuting journeys alike. Extensive city centre parking facilities, public and private bus routes, an underground system of 15 stations circling the Central Area and surburban rail services further enhance the accessibility of the City. Main line train services operate from the City's two major stations.

Glasgow Airport, 8 miles to the west of the City Centre, provides domestic and international flights to numerous destinations.Over 100 shuttle flights per week operate between Glasgow and London.

Once upon a bad time, all those travel arrangements made it easy to get out of Glasgow. Now, of course, it means that it is just as easy to arrive.

GLASGOW UNIVERSITY.

The BURRELL *Collection*

Almost, but not really, the best thing about the Burrell Gallery is the getting there. It sits romantically in the corner of a sloping field. It is spied through the surrounding chestnut, sycamore and ash trees. It is a small intimate place with a very big story to tell. It may be just three miles away from Glasgow's city centre, but it is of another world. And all because one man didn't like the game of cricket.

In 1867, the 15-year-old William Burrell was given a few shillings to buy himself a cricket bat. The young man spent the money on a painting. It was the start of one of the most extraordinary collections in the world – and it was Glasgow's great good fortune to acquire it. It was also, for many years, the city's biggest headache.

By the time he died, that collection had grown to some 8,000 objects, all beyond compare and many completely and utterly priceless. It became Glasgow's legacy, eventually. You can go and see it, absolutely free. Many people return again and again to dip into the collection, bit by bit. The alternative is to be overwhelmed.

Any catalogue gives only a boring idea of what Burrell was all about. He bought over 600 paintings in oils, watercolours and pastels. He was fond of Degas, Cézanne, Manet and Rembrandt. He purchased Chinese pottery, porcelain and jade, stained glass and tapestries. For over 80 years he cannily put together a collection of belongings so diverse and splendid that no-one was quite sure what to do with them. It took a similar feat of imagination and application to put them in a beautiful building in the corner of a field in Glasgow.

The Burrells owned ships. The family made fortunes. William Burrell decided to spend them seriously and cleverly on his works of art. But where eventually to put them became one of the city's longest-running serials during the 20th century. At many times, the story could have ended badly. Like a fairytale, the conclusion was happy, even joyous.

In 1944, Burrell gave his collection to Glasgow. The trouble was a stipulation which insisted that the gallery should be sited within 16 miles of the city and within four miles of Killearn, Stirlingshire. There was good reason for his geographical restrictions. His works demanded clean air and that was something, then, that Glasgow could not promise.

They haggled. In 1951, Sir William agreed to another site at the Dougalston Estate only seven miles out. But the National Coal Board said they were planning mining in the area. Once again, the scheme ground to a halt. Nearby Mugdock Castle was mentioned and then, in 1958 and at the age of 96, the collector died.

It was Government legislation which solved the problem. In 1956, the Clean Air Act was passed and the smog, the dirt and the pollution which hundreds of factories and shipyards had belched into the air quickly became a thing of the past. The sky could be seen at last.

A decade later the pieces began to fall into place and the works of art, which had been stored in warehouses, supposedly secretly, all over Glasgow, were moving closer to being put on view. Mrs Anne Maxwell MacDonald, daughter of the late Sir John Stirling Maxwell, the tenth baronet, gave the city an estate which had been in her family for 700 years and which was only three miles from the city centre. Burrell's trustees agreed – the collection had a potential home.

By 1972 – these matters seldom rush on apace – a young architect had been found to design the Gallery. Barry Gasson set to work. Five years later the money, some £21 million, was in place, and 12 months later the builders moved in. It took five years to complete the masterpiece.

The Burrell is not really a museum nor, in the strict sense, a gallery. It is a walk into someone's home. Sir William had insisted that incorporated into any scheme of things should be the reconstructed hall, drawing-room and dining-room of his beloved Hutton Castle near Berwick, where he lived.

His own home life was simple. He lived largely on porridge, although his guests were entertained more lavishly. But these three dark, wood-panelled rooms hint that for all his treasures, his domestic

style was frugal. It begs the question whether this austere man bought for the sake of buying, or for the sake of seeing. But the rooms have the Gallery, an integrity and justification. This was all the work of just one man.

Walk up to the front door, go past the wee bookstall that sells the pamphlets and posters, turn right and the first moment of excitement greets you. Sir William also left the city £450,000 towards the costs of building and the interest allowed the trustees to add other treasures. Here is the product of their taste, dramatically confronting the visitor.

It is the Warwick Vase, a huge 2nd century vessel unearthed near Rome 200 years ago by the Scottish painter and archaeologist Gavin Hamilton, the very object which Napoleon Bonaparte said he would acquire first if he ever conquered England. In 1979, it was bought for £253,808 to stop it from going to the Metropolitan Museum in New York. It is ironic that the place's most awesome exhibit was not collected by the man whose gallery this is. But Sir William Burrell would have wanted it this way.

That is just the start. Pass by those Hutton Castle rooms, mysteriously haunting – the lights were always turned off at the mains

by 10 p.m. every night – and look at the collection of oriental art. Chinese bronzes, jade and ceramics assault the eye daintily. Ming plates and vases abound. Go back a month later and see another collection because only 40 per cent of the Burrell can be seen at any given time.

Walk along the side of the gallery to inspect the oriental tapestries and rugs, which Burrell regarded as the best part of his collection. They hang on the walls in all their glory, originally from Persia.

Look the other way to see the stained glass, some 600 pieces, some incorporated into the main fabric of the building, some displayed internally and back-lit. The colours bounce at the eyes, even on those gloomy winter days when the trees hang sadly without their leaves and a low grey sky hangs over the city.

And then, at the far end of the gallery, are the paintings, a rich catholic selection of great artists, a Rembrandt there, given no special place of distinction, the Degas portrait of Edmond Duranty, Sisley's Bell Tower. It must be time for a cup of coffee, then retrace the steps to see the small priceless pieces that you have missed on you first trip around.

It is not difficult to say what this one magical Glasgow place has

done for the city. It has given the place confidence. At Kelvingrove, there is an Art Gallery that any European city would envy. But few can claim the leap of imagination which turned one man's lifetime of collecting into a palace for the people from whence he came. They talk many languages as they walk amongst the trees but the strongest dialect is Glaswegian. They go and keep coming back, for they have discovered a great secret.

Just about everything in the Burrell is something they would like to have in their own homes. It is full of carpets, tables, teacups, cutlery, crockery and pictures. Sir William Burrell's great distinction was that all the objects of art were genuine domestic artifacts. Their antiquity also teaches how people lived at home in different places around the world and at different times.

The Burrell Collection may have been created out of huge wealth and great artistic taste. It may have been placed in a Gallery full of space and air. But the word which sums it up is not to be found in the collection of artistic jargon. It just happens to be very "couthy".

SAUCHIEHALL
Street

At last, there is a Sauchiehall Street again. This is good news because it remains the centre of any Glasgow tourist route. The city's commercial fame may have been established by the great merchants and the big ships but throughout the world it was renowned because of a street with a funny name. It was a bit special, though, and its grandeur has come back.

Before they took the trams away Glasgow bustled and clanked, and nowhere more so than in Sauchiehall Street. The "caurs" would make their turn at Charing Cross and enter a long straight street that was a major thoroughfare and the home of big institutions.

About the name. It derives from the haugh of the sauchs, the meadow of the willows. That was why Kate Cranston, when she was creating her Willow Tea Rooms, asked Charles Rennie Mackintosh to use that tree as a design in the decorations. Now they might have to change that name to Maple Alley, or some such.

It was a street of food, theatre and fine shops. The Empire Theatre was there, the graveyard of English comedians whose humour refused to travel well north of Watford. Ferrari's was an eating-place when the city had few such establishments. The shops were household names – Pettigrew and Stephen's, Copland and Lyle's. There was the Locarno dance hall and later the Locarno Club, the epitome of raffishness. The Grand Hotel was, well, grand.

Sauchiehall Street was at turns both racy and reassuring. It may have lacked the sweeping lines of London's Regent Street or the sheer power of New York's Fifth Avenue, but it had a stature of its own that no other street in this city could match. There were fine shops in Renfield Street, Gordon Street was always busy and St Vincent Street

was solid. But Sauchiehall Street cornered the market in glamour.

The trams were the blood which flowed down this artery, and when they went the street looked positively anaemic. For 20 years it went nowhere in particular. The big stores closed, the theatre closed and there was more fast food than fine wine. In the gentrification of the New Glasgow, it was time to do something for such a lovely-sounding place.

It was the ten-year-old Norwegian maples which helped. Most Glaswegians will understand that all the best things in life mature when they are ten years old, or the best blends at least. The city bought 50 of them for a kick-off and planted them in nine-foot-deep pits. From such small maples, giant maples hope to grow.

There is, the way this city has developed, no aversion to prettiness. It is, after all, the dear green place, and the presence of so many florists in Glasgow is ample evidence that even urban man likes his flora and fauna. In spring, these maples announce the end of coldness with cream-coloured flowers. In autumn, they turn a burnished red and gold. They are going to grow to 40 feet, towering over the shoppers.

They added art deco seats and the whole lot cost £650,000 which was a bargain piece of beautifying. They kept the traffic away and they let Sauchiehall Street blossom again. In comparison to some of the other remarkable projects in the recent life of this city, it may not seem too dramatic. But it did at least prove there was new life in the old street again.

7 EATS

At One Devonshire Gardens Ken McCulloch is turning the rich and famous away from his small hotel with some aplomb. "I'm quite sure that Leonard Bernstein would like to stay here and we would love to have him. But we're full up that night." Of all the things which are making Glasgow newly famous, eating and sleeping may well top the list.

That night he will offer his diners some ritzy food. To start with, sir, the warm salad of scallops and ginger. Or maybe the avocado and smoked salmon with a dill mustard sauce? Or possibly the feuillette of chicken livers with almonds and cognac? The avocado and smoked salmon? Certainly, sir.

To follow, a little vegetable and coriander soup. For the main course there is a choice of stuffed saddle of lamb with redcurrant and rosemary, the breast of chicken with tarragon sauce, or, if you prefer to stay with the fish, we could offer you the rendezvous of seafood, cooked in a saffron and champagne sauce.

I'll show you the wine list – and for a sweet, there's tarte au citron, mousse brulée and our selection of cheeses is quite interesting tonight: brillat savarin, smoked cheddar or rolled oatmeal.

Glasgow always liked its eating. The lack of immigration posts at the border at Gretna Green meant that citizens journeying to see relatives living in England were always weighed down by suitcases full of the delicacies they missed – mutton pies, potato scones, spiced puddings. And there were seasonal treats as well. While England welcomed summer by going to Wimbledon or Glyndebourne, Glaswegians awaited the arrival in the M & A Brown's windows of the first crop of strawberry tarts with the dry flans, base of cream, a large

strawb covered with all that gooey red sticky stuff. Glasgow's notorious sweet tooth was satisfied by mountains of ice cream, double nougats (pronounced nuggets), McCallums (with the dod of raspberry sauce), 99's and Oysters.

If Glasgow did not invent fish and chips, it adopted them fiercely – and added pies, black puddings and haggis as alternative "suppers". Ladies took afternoon tea in Mrs Cranston's. Elegant diners would eat classically at the Malmaison, a French restaurant of impeccable distinction in the Central Station in the great days of the railways.

It took an outsider, a Greek called Reo Stakis, to understand that a Glaswegian's favourite tools were a knife and a fork. He started a social, if not quite a gastronomical, revolution by realizing that the city was prepared to put on its best clothes and go out and sit down and be served food. There are trendies now who would disparage the Stakis menu to be found in his places – prawn cocktail, well-done sirloin and black forest gâteau. But it was fun and for one generation, a marriage bureau.

At about the same time, Glasgow's students had discovered that academics do not march on empty stomachs and that the arrival of

Pakistanis in the city had brought it two Indian restaurants – the Shish Mahal and the Koh-i-Noor changed the diet of thousands. Now the list is endless. Pakoras, chicken tikkas, rogan joshes and prawn madrases may be the staple diet of part of Glasgow.

In fact, if Glasgow is a small Manhattan, it eats the same way. Pasta by the panful, doner kebabs by the sackload, chow mein with chopsticks. Italian, Turkish, Chinese and Indian foods have hijacked most of the local standbys. There is no longer a single place serving at lunchtime the businessman's delight, steak mince with an egg on the top. The city's taste-buds have become internationalized. Truly, we have all become citizens of the world.

At Enzo's, the man who owns it will simply insist you eat the mussels, or else. At the Caprese, if you don't know the Juventus score against Inter Milan, the portions might be smaller. Dino Zoff, the famous goalkeeper, ate in La Campagnola. From the Ad Lib to Zhivago's, the eaters' alphabet promises everything from hamburgers to haute cuisine.

You can drink too. In Glasgow a lot of people used to drink too much and many could still drink less. There are still in this city pubs whose drab bareness would be an affront to anyone whose intention

was to do anything other than get seriously "steaming". They are, happily, disappearing.

The trouble with Glasgow was that other people used to tell the ordinary guy when he could and could not drink. The law said at one time that all licensed premises should shut by nine o'clock of night. It became ten and then eleven. The customers were allowed ten minutes to drink up and that led to more problems. There used to be some unpretty sights after closing time.

There may still be, though not where most people go. Nowadays it is quite possible to drink for about 14 hours a day. The quirkiness of the Glasgow character has responded by deciding just whereabouts in that timescale he will take a refreshment and then take it gently.

He could go to a working man's pub where the talk will be about football and not much else, where the spirits are served in quarter-gill measures and where the choice of food is likely to be a pie or even a pie and beans, just possibly sober. He could take his choice of several blended whiskies, lager and beer. Or he could move upmarket and drink a café cognac to wash down his early morning croissants. The choice would be his and choice is something which he did not always have in the past.

CENTRE

Cars and their salesmen go there. Housebuilders and their buyers go there. Pop fans and boxing punters go there. Circus clowns and carnival seekers go there. On the motorways, signs signpost it miles before Glasgow gets better. It's so big that you cannot avoid it.

The Scottish Exhibition Centre is a prosaic name for a strictly functional structure that gave an old and useless part of Glasgow a new meaning. They painted it a very bright red to proclaim it a part of the New Glasgow which intends to stand up and shout for itself.

It needed something like that on the banks of the Clyde. Not only had the shipyards disappeared but the docks were in decline. The ferries to Belfast no longer ran from the Broomielaw. Only old grandfathers remembered the days when big liners left from their city to the New World. And there were no cargoes left to transport to the high seas. The Queen's Dock, once bustling, was left to die and then decompose.

Glasgow was left with a problem, or two problems. There was a crumbling site of some enormity which needed renewal. And there was a whole new type of economy which needed to be built as the city came to terms with a past which had gone and a present which needed to be created. The initials SEC were to become a well-known part of change and an end to decay.

Conferences attract people and people bring money. It has been shown to be big business from Zurich to Frankfurt, Paris to Milan. Why not Glasgow? So they built a conference pavilion which, when business wasn't being done, would be a pretty good place in which the likes of Elton John, Dire Straits and Miss Shirley Bassey could warble

to the enjoyment of a mere 10,000 who had bought tickets. So it had to be big.

Or rather, it had to be absolutely enormous. You could put an ice rink, the Burrell Collection, Lewis's store in Argyll Street and the Holiday Inn inside the SEC and there might still be a place for the odd restaurant or three. From one end of the site to the other, it's over half a mile.

It needs numbers to explain it. Its final cost was £36 million, its halls vary in size from 10,000 square feet to over 100,000 square feet and they can all be opened up to give an arena which, for example, allows 7,500 people to watch indoor football. It has 56 loos, five bars, two restaurants, a heli-pad and car parking for 4,000 cars.

Glasgow is still not quite sure what to make of the place. Curiously, for its size, it is quite well hidden, glimpsed over the wall from the Clydeside Expressway and seen briefly out of the corner of the eye from the Kingston Bridge. It is still fighting to win the hearts and minds of a generation of Glaswegians brought up on the homeliness of the old Kelvin Hall, where the kids went for the circus and the carnival every Christmas.

But the citizens will learn to love it as they go there to see such annual events as the Ideal Home Exhibition, where they even build brand new houses (four bedrooms and downstairs bath) and find them dwarfed under its massive ceilings. And the SEC houses major concerts, new sports. They've put a restaurant into the nearby Rotunda and a bridge across the river.

What it lacks is a nickname. Once someone has christened it, even rudely or cruelly, it will become part of the Glasgow folklore as well as a new bit of the landscape. Then its bigness will be seen as really beautiful.

The
SPORTING
Life

few days before war broke out, there was a football match at Hampden Park between Scotland and England. The result is totally irrelevant because England won. Its secure place in Glasgow folklore was established when a crowd of 149,269 turned out to watch the game. It still stands as the largest congregation of its type ever to watch grown men kick a ball in Europe.

Only in Brazil, where they love the game and have produced a few fair players, has that attendance record been beaten. There, they concreted a large hole in the ground, called it the Maracana Stadium and sometimes 200,000 watch matches. But none of the other 150 countries around the world which worship football can match Scotland's, and specifically Glasgow's, devotion to the game.

Rangers once drew 118,567 for just another League game against their arch-rivals Celtic. The city's smaller clubs have not been neglected. Clyde's record is 52,000, Partick Thistle can boast 49,838 and the amateurs of Queen's Park once drew 95,772. To be a Glaswegian who takes no interest in football is to be as rare as a politician who does not fancy power.

But in the New Glasgow, it is slightly different. People are not ashamed to admit that they like and even play badminton, judo, basketball, bowls, golf, volleyball or swimming. A world karate champion lives nearby. There are weightlifters, divers, joggers and horsemen. If football is the cardinal act of faith still, other sports do not lack adherents.

Even football, the grand old game, has changed – largely because it had to. In the not so good old days, it wove its magic over an audience without options. When there were shipyards and forges in the city, the working week ended at noon on Saturday. By some strange custom the city's womenfolk always tidied up the homes that afternoon. So a man had to stay away, have a couple of drinks and then join the dark swarms on their way to what was always called "ra gemme". There they were treated to great artistry on the pitch and poverty surrounding it. They stood on bleak terraces, open to the wind and the weather. In the case of Rangers and Celtic, the Old Firm, they shouted the obscenities of bigotry at each other. Toilet facilities were at best spartan, at worst non-existent. Women, sensibly, stayed away.

The numbers were so vast, no-one cared, certainly not the clubs. On one Wednesday night in 1970, Rangers played Bayern Munich in one European semi- final, Celtic played Inter Milan in another and at exactly the same time over 150,000 were standing watching. The tickets could have been sold twice over and that in a city whose population had shrunk to well under one million.

Glasgow, it has to be admitted, was a world leader in hooliganism. Now that curse has spread across large sections of mainland Europe. Glasgow, it can be proudly added, was also a world leader in tackling the problem and establishing a fragile peace. How this was done is a parable for a lot of what has changed here.

In 1980, Rangers played Celtic in the Scottish Cup final. It was a largely forgettable match which Celtic happened to win. The rival supporters came off the terraces to battle in the middle of the field and a serious, fatal riot was only averted by the entrance of mounted police. Those TV pictures went around a world which was forced to admit that Glasgow certainly had a very fine collection of mounted police, even if its football supporters were a disgrace.

In the aftermath, the act was thoroughly cleaned up. Alcohol was banned from the grounds and from the buses taking people there. At the same time, Rangers were building a new all-seated stadium, holding only 44,000 people. Slowly, by careful policing, the hooligans were driven away. Although an Old Firm match is still not a required stop by anyone of a sensitive nature, it need no longer be approached with a sense of deep foreboding.

There is no sign that football's importance is diminishing, largely because the game is played from Monday to Friday in the city's pubs. There football talk is big talk rather than small talk and anyone who doesn't know the name of Rangers' reserve centre is likely to be

THE TWO GREAT FORCES OF GLASGOW FOOTBALL COLLIDE, RANGERS V CELTIC.

THE TEMPLES OF GLASGOW'S OTHER RELIGION, IBROX IS SQUARE, PARKHEAD OVAL.

WEARING THE COLOURS. OPPOSING ENDS, CONTRASTING ALLEGIANCES.

condemned to a lifetime of solitary drinking.

But playing as well as performing happens to be fashionable again. For a while, the Glasgow marathon was the third largest event of its type in the world. It spawned legions of joggers who, every lunchtime, can still be seen sweating along the city streets. New sports halls encouraged mum and dad to take the children swimming. And new venues like the Scottish Exhibition Centre and the Kelvin Hall brought new indoor events for a city largely starved of watching top people in any sport apart from football.

Glasgow truly is sports-mad. When playing abroad in one of the big European football finals, Rangers and Celtic can always rely on 15,000 to 20,000 of their supporters to make the trip. One of the most popular programmes on Radio Clyde is its phone-in where the man on the terrace can air his views in public. "The Big Kick Off" is as eagerly awaited as it ever was. In its new-found eminence as a city which is taken seriously, the place is not about to abandon its oldest obsession. King Football Rules.

106

THERE IS LIFE AFTER FOOTBALL IN GLASGOW SPORT.   107

TRANSPORT
of Delight

It is Lilliput's answer to the Paris Metro. When it was built again, Glasgow bought it sight unseen at a price which had escalated to £35 million. They burrowed underground to see their old friend after its facelift and gave it the final accolade of approval. Henceforth the subway would be known as the Clockwork Orange.

Visitors rarely believe Glasgow has one. New York and Moscow have famous ones. Lots of other cities copied them. Places all over the world have ersatz ones which aren't quite the real thing because parts of them come up for air. But the Glasgow Underground was always the genuine article, slightly shrunk.

Its main virtue is that as an underground it is a carousel. It starts where it finishes and even if you don't get dizzy making the full circle, there are certainly bits of it which you never noticed. Like West Street, for example. What was – and might be again – so special about the subway is that Glaswegians may have lived on the other side of the Atlantic for 20 years but they still cannot get the smell of it out of their nostrils.

Radio Clyde once commissioned Matt McGinn to write a song about the subway. The rhymes would test Sammy Kahn. Starting from nowhere in particular, its place-names read – Buchanan Street, Cowcaddens, Kelvinbridge, Hillhead, Kelvinhall, Govan, Ibrox, Cessnock, Kinning Park, Shields Road, West Street, Bridge Street and St Enoch's. Kelvinhall used to be Partick Cross and Ibrox was Copland Road but they have gentrified the system.

It is the sixth-oldest subway in the world. When it was built in 1896, it cost £1,100,000. Since then passengers, about 14 million

every year, have travelled some 5,500,000 miles around the 6½-mile
stretch of track. Before it was done up in 1980, the tiny trains were a
thing of some splendour, the carriages made of teak and wonderfully
varnished, the seats of pure leather. It was by then a museum piece
which it is again today as a whole station stands as part of the display at
the city's transport museum in the Kelvin Hall.

It was the shoogle which made the Underground special.
Underneath the streets the subway went up and down. It was not a flat
mole-ride. The track jumped about, up and down and round and
round. Inside the carriages people were gently hurled about, something
which added to the friendliness of the city. It did wonders for a stricken
liver. The shoogle, sadly, has gone on the Clockwork Orange.

So, too, has the smell. Prosaically, it was in fact a mixture of
rusting cast iron, dampness and stale oil. It meant as much to the city as
the smell of the warm croissants on the terrace of the Café de la Paix. It
could be strongest sniffed at Kelvinbridge, where, presumably, the
nearby river added to its pungency. It was a familiar, not unpleasant,
smell.

113

In 1980, after many delays, the subway was refurbished and reopened by the Queen. Before, it had taken 28 minutes to complete the circle but now it whizzes you round in 22 minutes. The orange trains are still as small, but cleaner. There is no smoking allowed now. The 33 trains work six days a week and are given a rest on Sunday.

In almost a century it may have established one grim record for the world's subways. In all that time, only one person has died in front of a train, and that was an accident. Maybe Glaswegians revere it too much to be giving it a bad name.

We like our Underground. From down below it tells you a lot

114

about what is happening up above. South of the Clyde it is largely deserted. Traffic between St Enoch's and Hillhead is busier with students and shoppers. Some people only like travelling clockwise or anti-clockwise. It is a subway with a heart.

There is a story that because all the station platforms are in the middle, with the trains arriving at either side, one side of every carriage was never seen by the public and was therefore left unpainted. It cannot be true because no-one would treat it that shabbily. It's the city's little secret and since its facelift it's more Orange than Clockwork.

THE RIVER CLYDE CUTS GLASGOW IN HALF. THE CITY'S SOUTH SIDE STILL REMAINS MUCH OF A MYSTERY TO THOSE WHO WERE BROUGHT UP IN THE NORTH. CONSIDERING THAT IT WAS, OVER THE CENTURIES, THE CRADLE OF HALF A DOZEN INDUSTRIES WHICH HAD A WORLDWIDE IMPACT, THE CLYDE IS AN INTIMATE LITTLE RIVER. IT SQUIRMS ITS WAY THROUGH THE CITY AND THE BRIDGES ARE SHORT AS WELL. ONLY DOWNSTREAM, GLIMPSING AT THE HILLS DOES IT GUSH FORWARD IN SOME MAJESTY.

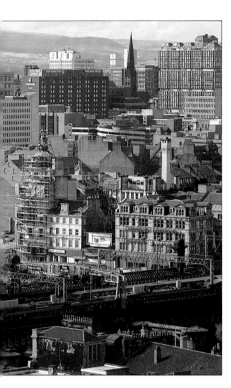

119

11 SPEAKEASY

I t is a monstrous calumny put about by outsiders that it is as difficult to understand a Glaswegian as a native-born Himalayan. Help ma Boab, it's enough to make you boak. It's as big a lie as those who claim that the whole city is made up of wee punters who are always stotious.

People are always breenging into our business. Even if you're doing no more than lying in your scratcher, someone will be saying that you're oot bevvying. I get black affronted at that kind of thing. Bawheids. Anyway, as far as the patter is concerned, out our way we're awfully pan loaf. What they say is mince.

One of the best-selling books in the city over the last few years was a little paperback published by the Glasgow District Libraries entitled *The Patter*. It sold, to everyone's surprise, in the sort of numbers usually associated with Mr Harold Robbins. It was a dictionary of the Glasgow patois.

It is true that in Glasgow there is a denseness and a richness about the way people talk. There are certain words and phrases which are found nowhere in the rest of the world other than alongside ten miles of the banks of the River Clyde. But most of the time, its people talk good English with the occasional glottal stop. It is not a city where a visitor needs the local equivalent of an Intourist guide just to understand the natives. The most difficult Glaswegians to understand are the genteel ladies of Kelvinside who speak with plums in their mouths.

The whole point about the Glasgow dialect and its indigenous sayings is that you don't have to understand them in detail because the sound or inflection will give you the drift straightaway. For example, a nippy sweetie is a nippy sweetie. It means sharp tasting, but it also

describes a certain sort of lady with a scorching tongue. If you have any trouble understanding a Glaswegian, tell him to stop being a nippy sweetie.

Oiling the New
GLASGOW

O n 10 March 1988, at a meeting of the Institution of Structural Engineers, 11 Upper Belgrave Street, London SW1X 8BH at 6 p.m., a paper was delivered by T Ridley, BSc, CEng, FIStructE, FICE, FASCE, FRSE, and D S Blackwood, who has to be content with a BSc, CEng, FIStructE, FICE. It began . . .

The expansion of service industries in the city centre of Glasgow has been seen as one of the best ways of achieving the future economic potential which has been identified in recent development studies. This economic regeneration has followed in the wake of successful political efforts to show that Glasgow can succeed in overcoming its historically bad image with bold and imaginative projects aimed at attracting major investment from both the public and private sectors. Quite remarkably, there is now a spirit of confidence which is reflected in the style of its promotional slogans such as Glasgow's Miles Better, Glasgow Can Do It and Glasgow Action. The spirit is now bringing about a large number of exciting projects which demand the most challenging responses . . .

OK, so it's not very racy, but it's clearly stated and quite important. Now read on.

During the early 1970s there was the dawn of a new industrial age in Scotland when large quantities of oil and gas were found under the seabed of the hostile North Sea. Harnessing these natural resources of energy has proved to be a challenge of technology for which considerable vision and imagination has been required . . .

So just what has this got to do with the New Glasgow? The Britoil Headquarters, that's what it's got to do with the New Glasgow. That

glass building, just as you come off the M8 slip road, just before you reach the Albany Hotel, on the same side as Habitat.

This area of land had previously been occupied by a group of old buildings which had been acquired to allow the construction of the M8 motorway to take place during the late 60s. The decision to locate the new headquarters building here has thus achieved the redevelopment of the area which otherwise had become an eyesore in the city centre during the years since completion of the motorway . . .

I've seen it, pal, very cute, nice little place, but what's so special about it?

The Britoil headquarters building ranks as probably the largest recent UK office building for accommodating a single organisation. The main pedestrian entrance is from St Vincent Street. In addition to the main foyer and mall, with lift and escalator access to the upper levels, this level also accommodates conference facilities, a medical suite, a large staff restaurant, and office space. Externally, the building is clad in high quality, low maintenance materials consisting of polished granite

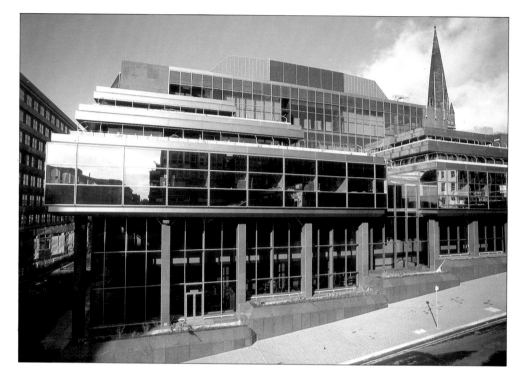

cladding to the walls and column surfaces and glazed curtain walling comprising double glazed solar control reflective glass panels in aluminium frames. Internally, the finishes are also of high quality with carpeted raised flooring used extensively in conjunction with proprietary relocatable partitions and suspended ceilings . . .

So it's smart, they don't have a canteen and there's enough glass to build a thousand greenhouses. There's more.

The building took three years to complete at a construction cost of £35.9 million. It required 1.5 million man hours to do so. The first sod was cut on 11 September 1983 and it was officially opened by the Scottish Secretary of State Malcolm Rifkind on 19 December 1986.

At its peak, 470 men were employed in the construction and 42 of the 64 contractors were Scottish. Ten thousand tonnes of cement were used and the building is believed to be the largest private office development in Scotland with a gross floor area of 492,000 square feet. Inside 90,000 carpet tiles have been laid and 4,000 metres of wall

partitioning erected. The computer and communication services require 130 miles of cabling. Between them, the computers carry out seismic interpretation, reservoir simulation, analysis of offshore structures, economic evaluation and various accounting functions.

The building also includes a feature clock designed and built by Alan Hamshere of Gateside in Fife. Weighing over 700lbs, it took 15 months to complete. The clock tells the time in 24 countries across the globe and also the times of high tide on the Clyde. It also, amongst other things, shows the position of the sun and the moon in the celestial sphere and zodiac.

Over 700 staff are currently housed in the building.

Very impressive. I'm Taurus, will that clock tell me my horoscope?

I wouldn't imagine so but you've missed the point.

What's that?

Where is it, pal? Not in London, not in Edinburgh, but here in Glasgow.

The
EAST END

Two nice Englishmen – and this is a very true story – came to work in Glasgow and as the leaves began to blossom one spring, their minds turned to thoughts of . . . believe it or not, cricket. The new season was approaching, they felt the need for some practice, so they took their bats, their ball, and their wickets down to Glasgow Green one lunchtime and in a quiet corner of this dearest of all dear places in the city, they managed an hour of quite strenuous training.

Naturally, they were thirsty and decided to repair to the nearest pub in London Road, a den some distance away from those kind of establishments sought out by Mr Egon Ronay's inspectors. A Glaswegian who accompanied them was sure that they would be allowed a pint in peace, despite their accents, but taking cricket bat, ball and wickets into such a pub could be tricky. These sporting implements could well be construed as offensive weapons because cricket was not too well understood in these parts of the city.

He was totally wrong. They ordered two pints of heavy. "Been practising your cricket, pal?" asked the barman. Before long a spirited argument had broken out about the relative merits of Mr Ian Botham and other members of the England XI who were at that time engaged in a Test series with the West Indies. So impressed was one of the cricketers that soon afterwards he bought a smashing wee Barratt house which overlooked Glasgow Green. The pub became his local and he claimed that nowhere on earth – and he had been about a bit – had he found such strenuously argumentative companionship. And nobody stole his bat either.

The East End has always been Glasgow's Achilles' heel. If the whole city was once a workshop, the East End was its foundry, a hot, steaming mass of machinery and people. It was a stone's throw from where the Gorbals was until they knocked the whole place down. The great factories, the Clyde Iron Works, the Tollcross Tube Works, Parkhead Forge and Sir William Arrol's had all disappeared. What was left was a vast suppurating boil on the face of an otherwise good-looking city. Land was left derelict, slums fell down. Those who lived there lived very badly indeed. The whole place was not just a health hazard but an affront to decent humanity.

Praise be, the politicos rolled up their sleeves and didn't wash their hands. They swung into top gear, establishing the Glasgow Eastern Area Renewal project, the largest of its kind in Europe. Now, to see if the people who live there like the place, you have to fight your way past delegations speaking funny languages and coming from all over the world to steal its ideas.

The East End is not, and never will be, a garden suburb. But it has become a bright and lively place where anyone would be happy to live. In the ten-year period between 1977 and 1986, publicly and privately, they spent some £292 million on housing alone. But they threw not just money at the place, they sowed the seeds of simple common sense.

What do you want of a community? A decent place to live, good schools for the kids, some trees and open spaces, good shops and above all helpful and friendly neighbours. That mixture had never been attained when, a generation previously, they had decanted the less well-off to Easterhouse and Drumchapel, still some kind of cultural Sowetos which must be the next aim of this city to improve.

In the East End, it has been different, a wonderful mixture of Glasgow's best bits. The Barras, the open-air market, remains untouched. But up the road Bridgeton Cross has been given a shopping centre which might become the envy of Newton Mearns. They have been trying to bring work to the area so it once again becomes a self-contained part of Glasgow, fiercely independent, a law unto itself. Gardens are landscaped. Parkhead, Dalmarnock and Bridgeton will have been completely reborn – and Glasgow will be well rounded again.

Holiday in
GLASGOW

T he late Sir Hugh Fraser, who had inherited the city's finest outfitters from his father, once opened a new men's boutique quite near to Slater's, down on the waterfront at the bottom of Jamaica Street. The windows were stuffed with the best Messrs Dior, St Laurent and Gucci could send to Glasgow. It was some time before the news was broken to Sir Hugh that everyone went to Howard Street. He retreated.

Slater's isn't just the best-known tailors in town – it's also a vital part of the tourist route and some of the signs inside it are written in Icelandic. They arrive in their droves every weekend, having been informed of Slater's by adverts placed in the Reykjavik newspapers. If Glasgow thinks the shop is full of bargains, the Icelandic exchange rate must appear to the tourists as if he's more or less giving the stuff away.

Glasgow, even without the Garden Festival, even without the tag as European Capital of Culture, has found in the last decade that tourists want to share the enjoyment of the city with those of us who live here. In 1982 only 700,000 holidaymakers had stopped in Glasgow. Six years later that figure had risen to four million. Nine out of every ten of them came from England. The four Icelandic flights were a nice little bonus.

On average, if there is an average tourist, he will spend about £150 during his stay. That means that Glasgow will be about £600 million better off from its visitors. As importantly, the city tourist trade probably stacks up some 5,000 jobs which would not have been there before.

There are a couple of well-trodden tourist routes. Going east from

the city centre, the cameras click at Provand's Lordship, the only pre-Reformation dwelling-house left in the city, built in 1471, originally part of a poorhouse. Opposite, the neglected Glasgow Cathedral, built on a site which has been a place of worship since AD397. On to the Western Necropolis, a model of the Père Lachaise Cemetery in Paris, overlooked by the statue of John Knox. The guide leads them on to the People's Palace, the old Templeton's carpet factory, designed along the lines of the Doge's Palace in Venice. Take a quick spin through the Barras, do another wee bit of shopping in the Briggait, the reconverted Fishmarket. Have a peek at the SV *Carrick*, now the home of the Royal Naval Volunteer Reserve Club of Scotland, but the ship which still holds the sailing record of 65 days for the 12,000-mile passage from Adelaide in Australia to London. Turn back into the shops, gaze under the Hielanman's Umbrella, the favourite meeting-place for out-of-towners, cut back to have a look at the Trades House in Glassford Street, designed by Robert Adam and opened in 1794, and complete the journey by enjoying the sight of the City Chambers, 100 years old and the finest piece of Victorian architecture in Glasgow.

Or you could go west to see the Theatre Royal at the top of Hope Street, the Glasgow School of Art, designed by Rennie Mackintosh, the Mitchell Library and on to Park Circus with its curved terraces, the original homes of some of Glasgow's wealthiest merchants. And sit in Kelvingrove Park alongside the University and see the river below you and the sweep of the Renfrewshire hills on the far side before taking an ice cream in the University Café in Byres Road.

Of an evening, watch a production at the Citizens Theatre, founded in 1942 by the playwright James Bridie, or go to the Theatre Royal, home of the Scottish Opera. Or, if it is the right time of the year, do not miss the Pavilion's couthy pantomime.

Shop the next day in Buchanan Street, take a run out to the zoo or have a game of golf. Relax and keep your fingers crossed that the rain stays off. Sleep well in your hotel.

THE 1988 GLASGOW GARDEN
FESTIVAL BROUGHT FLOWERS
AND MUCH MORE TO THE CITY.
THE BELL'S BRIDGE GAVE ITS
PEOPLE ANOTHER WAY TO GO
FROM ONE SIDE OF THE RIVER TO
ANOTHER. FOR A FEW MONTHS THE
CLYDESDALE TOWER HOISTED
ALOFT SEARCHERS AFTER A
BIRD'S EYE VIEW OF THE PLACE.
MOSTLY PEOPLE LAUGHED AND
SMILED ON A PATCH OF
RECLAIMED WASTELAND.

THE BOTANIC GARDENS.

FLYING HIGH

I pass my favourite place almost every day in life. Only occasionally am I flush enough or fortunate enough to go in and out of it. Glasgow Airport at Abbotsinch mostly makes me a road hazard to other Renfrewshire commuters.

Coming into town down the M8, my eyes will wander left and stay there, to gaze at the rows of sleek 757s, the dumpy wee Loganair buses and the bulging twin-engined Boeings. My steering becomes erratic, my neck cricked. For anyone who would be a nomad, the place is an adult's secret garden.

As airports go, it's more of a Viscount than a Jumbo, small and comfortable. It's not at all like the Charles de Gaulle in Paris where they process you through plastic tubes. Its duty free shop is like a corner shop compared to Schipol's equivalent of the travelling man's Harrods. It could do with some of the vastness of empty space which greets you in Rio. At least its baggage handling is better, marginally, than at Cairo where all the cases spew up one tunnel. It's not a federal city of separate burghs like JFK, nor as huge as Dallas or Chicago's O'Hare. It's a lot cleaner than Prague but doesn't serve those lethal planter's punches which eliminate jet lag and disconnect the central nervous system on arrival at Antigua.

Such effortless place-dropping may only serve to invite a place in pseuds' corner, and to be honest I haven't been everywhere, man, and more's the pity because I'd like to go to every last airport in the world. And come home to dear old Abbotsinch.

Old hands who remember British Imperial Airways are fond of saying that flying isn't what it used to be, that one is thrown capriciously through the corridors rather than cosseted as a first-class élite. Maybe so, but there is nothing like going to catch a plane, even in Glasgow's Shuttle Lounge.

The mere excitement means you forget on return exactly where in that bleak NCP car park you have left the motor. Stepping through the puddles (it's always raining when you come back to Abbotsinch) trying to find the wheels only adds to the feeling that flying into Glasgow has been fun.

Why – thinking about it – does one always believe that before stepping into an aircraft at Glasgow, it is necessary to buy four morning papers, the latest trashy paperback and yet another disposable lighter? Yet it always seems to be so.

Then there are the people to watch. Lance Corporals of industry with the plastic attaché cases, the captains of commerce striding towards the waiting limo. Young girls with overnight bags on the way to their lovers. Maw, Paw and the weans back from Benidorm with enough luggage to make sure that Captain Scott came back from the Pole with his feet warm.

I go to watch them sometimes with my own children, who are fascinated by the size of the sticky buns in the cafeteria, the price of which would bring tears of disbelief to the eyes of an Arab street trader. They ask where this plane is going and that one and can we go on that one, and if I had the money we probably would and not come back for a while. I'm training them to be worldly, without leaving the coffee shop.

By comparison, the other Scottish airports are two-engined prop jobs. Prestwick makes me feel lonely and I hope that British Midland gets the nod to fly transatlantic from Abbotsinch because I want to see the Jumbos on my way home to the mince and tatties. Edinburgh's clean but empty, Aberdeen's a wee appendage to the helicopter business. I've always wanted to fly from Dundee, though.

To where? I have become increasingly fascinated at Glasgow by those little flights which creep in and out, hopping over the perimeter road. The ones to Islay and Lerwick, Inverness and the Western Isles, places much nearer home but mostly unseen by the passenger down the international departure channels. They are the little arteries to the heart of a small country of unrelated villages.

That's the Abbotsinch secret, this blending of the big birds going continental and the wee sparrows hopping from landing-strip to landing-strip. That's why it's such a homely place.

Once, I returned from a golfing holiday in Spain, totally wrecked. A minibus awaited and in the confusion of boarding I left duty frees (important) and passport (not totally essential) lying on the pavement. An hour later I rang to report the loss. Next day they told me a porter had handed them in to security. I went to security, picked the articles up, and left a fiver for the porter. A month later this honest man came up to me and thanked me and said that I shouldn't have bothered. That really made it, for me, *Glasgow's* Airport.

GOOD NIGHT GLASGOW . . .